This Chick Got Baggage

INTRODUCTION:

This Chick Is One Badass Ninja!

Yea, I got baggage. But, I'm not asking you to help me carry it. Just don't stand in my way, looking at me all-stupid in my face. If you're not going to help me- I would politely ask that you move the fuck out of my way, so I can carry it my damn self. (insert eye roll here).

Table of Contents

Fallen

I have fallen more than once, and I picked myself up out of the darkness each time. My baggage is living proof that I was there. Now I carry it cloaked with strength and resilience. ~ Arena Horn

My Crown Slipped

For seven years I taught "Financial Coaching & Case Management." I have also completed facilitation training in "Controlling Anger & Learning to Manage It" (CALM).

"Batterers Education Program" (BEP) & "Women's Moving On" for the State of Iowa Department of Correctional Services.

I enjoyed empowering people and encouraging positive cognitive change. I believe that we are all capable of change, and I'm living proof!

During that time I had the opportunity to work with both sides- The Victim, and the Batterer. I learned their thought process. I heard the stories from the Victims & Batters. Those stories helped me learn to understand, it was not my fault. I learned to forgive him and, most of all to forgive myself.

With domestic violence, you begin to question your self-worth. You begin to believe you are insignificant.

The batterers have to tear you down! They strip you of your morals and values, just to begin their grooming process.

They start by building you up. They put you on a pedestal. They make you feel like the world revolves around you. They buy you nice gifts. They say everything you want to hear.

They start verbally abusing you. They push limits just to see how far they can go. Then, they punch you in your face. They attack your soul. Those hands that once provided you security and comfort- are now the hands that inflict the pain.

The sweet nothings that he once whispered in your ear- with his soft voice now scream that you're worthless. The vibrations of the damaging words hit your face like stone punches.

When he's done with these things, he looks at you with those eyes and begs for your forgiveness. You forgive him, and then the cycle begins. He has you hooked.

Soon you become just as dark and empty as he is. But, let me tell you the most important factor in all this. Anything, that is torn down can be built back up! You are beautiful, worthy, you have a purpose, you're amazing, a survivor, and a worrier!

So today, if your crown has been knocked off stand up, pick it up, place your crown back on, and walk in your damn purpose!

The Love I Need

"Love and how we feel we need to be loved," is a different experience for each individual. We all have our own distinct requirements. I don't regret my love experiences. I would endure the good, bad, and ugly all over again.

Especially, if I knew it would lead me to exactly where I am today. When I define what I need love to look and feel like for me; I know that I need it to make me smile, laugh, and cry. It needs to contain honesty and integrity.

Realistically, it will have highs and lows. Love will never be abusive. Sexual boundaries will be adhered to, respect will be given and received. My love will thrive from admiration, communication, and compromise.

My Baggage Synopsis: I'm not shitting sparkles and glitter here!

I'll start with this: My baggage is messy and full as fuck. Don't let it fool you—it appears to be Louis Vuitton at first sight. But, when you open it up, it's clear as hell that this shit came straight from Walmart.

I have no idea what I'm doing. I stopped striving for perfection. I realized it didn't exist. Believe me I realized that hard and fast at birth. I was born a bastard child, placed in the arms of a black teenage mother.

My family's journey started rough. My parents provided my sister and I with everything we needed. They strove to do better because they wanted us to have better. They wanted to get us off of the welfare cycle and into a more thriving environment.

They didn't want us to continue to fall victim to the thieves that lurked in the night. You know the kind to take whatever they could get their filthy hands on. Disregarding the heartache and feelings of violation they caused. The dope heads would look for a crumb as they itch at the scabs on their faces.

There was this white van that sold boosted items cheap. Not to mention this funny smell that crawled through the vents and doorways. There was this fight that broke out in the parking lot. The next day we discovered a tooth lying in the dried up crusted puddle of blood. The old men and older boys whistling at us and calling us baby. Eww!

They would offer us candy with Lucifer's intentions, attempting to lure us to an area where no one could see.

I would hold my little sister's hand tight to ensure she arrived home safely from school. Never letting her see the fear in my own eyes. I carried a small stick in my hand just in case I had to fight off dogs.

As we headed down the staircase I could see our back slab of cement. I knew we were almost safe. I'll never forget hurrying her home one day- I could hear the boys' voices from behind. They would call me names because I wouldn't let them sneak a peek.

As the tears made their way down my face, I would tell my little sister to skip to get her to move a little faster. Once we made it inside the door, I locked it and put the chain lock on. I looked out a few times to make sure they were gone.

After we moved and adjusted to being in a predominantly white neighborhood, things were good and had been for a while. I had goals. I had been working at my job for 4 years. I had track dreams. I was going to start college at the University of Northern Iowa.

Then I came face to face with the darkness again. This time the darkness would bring with it a pain of unknowable depth. Physically and verbally violent relationships tear you down to irrelevance fast and make you question your existence.

I would go through everything I have been through, just to be the person I am today. The joy, sorrow, and the really tough shit that caused me to ugly cry. I'm not perfect. I would still take this mess as is. No refund needed! My journey has taught me how to love, and how I want to be loved. Also, to never take anything for granted. My journey has taught me patience and to keep loving. My journey has taught me that I want to keep moving forward.

I can honestly say I have endured some of life's hardest obstacles. I'm sure that statistically speaking; I'm a walking red flag. A relationship expert would probably label me as unfriendable, undateable, unwifeable, and unable to adopt a dog. But with the right lover and a dash of self-love, I'm able to say I'm crushing it!

If I'm keeping it real, I have to admit—at times I've been a bad wife, mother, daughter, sister, aunt, and friend. I've been hungry, beaten, and broke. I've been cheated on and I've cheated. I've been molested and raped. I've given birth, miscarried, given birth again. I've been a single mother on welfare.

I've been physically assaulted. I've been the assaulter. I've been lied to, and I've been the liar. I've been bullied! I've also been the bully in the past. I've struggled with my mental health. I even struggle to this day. (There is no handbook).

If I'm going to keep it real with the negatives, I'll also keep it real with the positives. I'm a great wife, mother, daughter, sister, aunt, and friend. I've been a motivator, a warrior, and a survivor. I've made people laugh and I've been there to wipe away tears.

I've been a supporter, caretaker, and facilitator. I've listened without judgement. I build people up, encourage them, and empower them. I've given everything I had, even when I had nothing left to give. I'm empathetic and I love hard.

I'm able to say I'm sorry, and learn from my mistakes. I wake up every day and walk in my purpose.

I'm proud that I strive to be the best version of myself every day. I'm a work in progress, and I'm still writing my story that I never want to end.

We All Have Baggage: If someone tells you different, they are a damn liar!

Everyone has some sort of baggage. Our past decisions, values, and circumstances lead us to exactly where we are in the journey called life. The first step in claiming your baggage is when you see it coming around that baggage claim. You pick that shit up with both hands and start walking.

Don't look away from it or wait for it to pass. Pick that shit up and own it! No matter how ugly it is. If you or your partner can't identify, accept, and conquer; your baggage your relationship is doomed. We have to put in the work to get the results we want, and the relationships we deserve.

Our own insecurities will drive our partners away. Control issues, jealous rages, and clinginess will drain the life out of a relationship, fast! Find assistance if you need to address some issues and put your insecurities to rest. You don't need others to validate your existence.

If you or your partner has commitment issues; or, if one is falling faster than the other -Again, draw your line. You don't want to dedicate five years to a relationship that's at a standstill. Or, to a relationship that isn't moving in the direction you want.

Relationships often start with a honeymoon stage. During which, everyone is on their best behavior. It can take time to see a person's true colors. I'm just saying! If you're going full speed ahead make sure your partner isn't still at the starting line. Inventory your relationship from time to time. Be sure they are taking some steps in the right direction.

Trust is the core of any relationship. When it is destroyed, the bond begins to crumble. Every relationship has its own dos and don'ts, depending on the people involved. Have a conversation about what is acceptable and what is not. Your beliefs and values are very important to discuss before a line is crossed. It's hard to bounce back once someone feels betrayed. Laying things out beforehand can help avoid crushing your core. Also, it is setting you up to build on a solid foundation.

You don't want to bring drama into a new relationship. Sort as much of that shit out as you can, before starting a new one. Being messy as fuck, will interfere with a new relationship and cause undue stress. Take the time to heal and do some self-reflecting.

Guilt Baggage: We are guilty of a shit show!

As humans, we have all been offensive or broken a law. We all experience guilt and no one is exempted. Well, maybe not a crazy ass narcissist they tend to lack the feeling of guilt and remorse, but speaking of the average person who has a heart.

We are human, we make mistakes. We feel guilty when we have wronged someone or acted out of character. Guilt is a normal emotion although it can be paralyzing for some to experience.

The problems surface when you carry around guilt for too long months or even years. Some quilt can cause effects as soon as minutes after experiencing it. I have hurled a dinner or two over guilt. We hang onto our guilt because we want to punish ourselves but that's not how you make things right. We have to stop Stewing in our guilt soup. Make things right and keep it moving. Stop the self-judgment, Stop the fucking should a, would a, could a, and forgive yourself! Stop Sulking in your shit put your big girl panties on and seek forgiveness from those you have wronged!

Fear Baggage: Throat punch fear in and show it who's boss!

OK so I'm not talking about the heebie-jeebies I get when I see ugly ass raccoons or the slow-motion gasp I have at the thought about falling flat on my face in public. I'm talking about the paralyzed feeling you get when you're facing the unknown. When the potential of failure is staring at you straight in the face, when you are frozen, find the courage deep within and throat punch!

For me, the mere sight of a snake can take my breath away and cause the world to close in around me. There are certain intimidating situations and people who can coward us with just a glance, kick that asshole in the balls!

If you allow your fears to run shit, it will trap you inside your own head and prevent you from enjoying life and living in the moment. Don't let fear win! You don't want to miss out on your journey, so karate chop Felicia in the knee caps and tell that bitch bye!

It's OK to be uncomfortable. If you want to be free from fear acknowledge what you're feeling and kick its ass. Don't let it hold you hostage. Move slowly but always be moving forward reaching what you thought was once impossible, and that's how fucking QUEENS are made and dreams come true!

The Ex Baggage: When you close the door on a relationship, be sure to leave the baggage with them.

I always knew when I was about to pay for it. Moving in closer to me each time, he asked me what the fuck I was thinking. I looked down at his hands. The hands he had once used to hold me that had provided me so much pleasure—now he used them to inflict pain upon me. His hands were now balled into fists, his face gathering that lunatic look.

When I still refused to answer his questions, he grabbed me by the neck and pushed me up against the wall. He was so strong! Especially, when he was in a rage. I felt helpless. My mind started spinning, and I thought to myself,

"*Why is he doing this to me?* " I started crying uncontrollably.

I was searching his eyes, searching for something; But I found nothing. Just empty blackness and hatred. When his grip let up for a second, I twisted free and started running down the hall. He ran after me and grabbed me by my dress.

I lost my footing and fell to the floor. Shocking pain blasted through my body.

I curled into the fetal position, attempting to protect and console my throbbing belly. My belly that was carrying his flesh, his child. He calmly stepped over me and dragged me down the hall by my hair.

I could feel it pulling out of my scalp as blood trickled down my forehead. He shut me in the bathroom and held the knob so I couldn't get out. I just cried! A scream tore through me like a shard of glass. I pounded and kicked the door until I had nothing left. No one was coming to save me from him.

After a while, he opened the door and let me out. He wrapped his arms around me, kissed me on the top of my head. He told me that he loved me, and that he was sorry. I needed to understand where he was coming from, and he'd needed to make a point. What he had just done didn't faze him a bit. The look in his eyes revealed not an ounce of repentance. His eyes that I would get lost in showed nothing. Just a blank soul.

Self Love

Your wrath showed me how I don't want to be loved...Because I love myself, I know what love should feel like.

Arena Horn

Emotional Baggage: Don't let your past define you!

We all have experienced some type of toxic relationship. Whether it be a friendship, kinship, or romantic relationship. These early relationships mold us to what we become to expect of our relationships. You may have been verbally abused, abandoned, cheated on, or even physically abused. Don't let your past intrude on your current relationships or it wins.

My abuser is dead. Uninvited, He still haunts me. His actions have left impressions that will forever intrude on my being. I often still experience emotional relapses that expose glimpses of irrationality, instability, insecurity, and isolation.

A woman recovering from a broken heart is often misconstrued as a psychotic bitch. What people fail to realize is often we are shattered into a million pieces and left trying to fit them back together alone. We are hurtful to others only because we want someone else to hurt, just as much as we do.

We often self-sabotage new relationships. Testing boundaries; pushing to see what type of reaction we get. Not realizing the damage we are doing to others. This leaves us with our own mirror images, looking back at us as ugly monsters. We are embarrassed and ashamed. Those emotions are often masked by anger.

He never gave up on me. He always assured me that he loved me- for *me*! I was a good-hearted person he could see that in me. The person he knew deep down in his heart I would return to be. So he waited patiently, never pushing but always standing there as comfort and support.

Boy oh Boy, did he have a wait in front of him. I don't think he truly knew what he was getting himself into. I made him wait. I took a long time to deal with the aftermath of my prior relationship. Although, I was no longer in imminent danger, my ex continued to disturb my thoughts uninvited. Even as dead as he lays, due to a self-inflicted gunshot wound to the head.

I often found myself doing things to get that rush and excitement of something new. It was a false temporary feeling of pleasure, bliss, and love. To recreate these feelings I got tattoos, bought a house (I was not ready for), and changed cars like I did shoes. I even got dogs I was not prepared to take care of.

I hosted extravagant birthdays for my daughter just to see her smile. I would do anything that I could to ease the pain. I was searching for something to bring me happiness. These smiles and feelings were evanescent. After the newness wore off- I was often left with emptiness. I didn't understand that I needed to find joy in my purpose. My happiness was a state of well- being, which was attributed to an artifact.

I learned that once I was in love and gave myself time to heal; I could revitalize my sexual being. Once I found my love and soul mate, I truly knew the terms and conditions of the love I wanted. My sexual experience would be like nothing I had ever encountered. I had to forgive myself, and let go of the past- so that I could move forward.

Remember you can't truly be in love, if you're loving out of fear.

It's You: Own your shit!

Own your stank-ass shit. Stop pussyfooting around you are emotionally unstable and you need to fix that shit! What I'm saying is if you long to be the bride but are always the bridesmaid-

Or, if your relationships always end in "It's not you; it's me," then something's wrong!

Every relationship you have is unstable, unhealthy, and ugly as fuck; hmm, might be you?

Or, if you go through friends like tampons—sweetheart, it's definitely you.

Some people are content with being alone. There is absolutely nothing wrong with that. For that you get two snaps and a circle! You should never feel like anything is wrong with you for wanting to be alone—

point blank, period. Being alone allows for self-inventory and healing.

Society makes us feel like we are insignificant or something is wrong with us if we are not married by a certain age. We feel bad if we are divorced, or single for too long! That is just bullshit! My friend, let me look at some "Plenty Of Fish" selections and . . . umm, well? Let's just say there are some unique motherfuckers on there. The site has a lot of shit to sift through. So, I totally get why some opt to remain single. If being single is what you want that's absolutely ok.

Our insecurities are good for nothing except self-sabotaging and creating self-doubt. It's hard to bounce back if your heart was broken due to infidelity. Even living in fear from a wrath of terror. You have to remember love is real and it can exist for you with the right person.

You will definitely go through some bad before you get to the good. But, it's so worth it. When you actually find the love you deserve! You don't want to run a good mate off-

due to episodes of psychotic paranoia and erratic emotional instability.

If a person has done nothing to betray your trust; treating them like they have will run them off fast as roaches run when the lights come on. So don't allow yourself to breach their privacy. Never deny them the room to breathe.

Nothing wrong with setting boundaries, especially when you sit down and do it together. Discuss things: like the way certain actions they make you feel. Together you can understand what each of you needs to have a healthy and successful relationship.

Namaste Bitches: Know your self-worth and settle for nothing less!

Do you, boo! Our thoughts are intrusive, but they will only be given power if we give in to them. Replace negative intrusive thoughts with powerful statements and affirmations.

The most motivating power in life is our thoughts. Thoughts can never be taken from us. How you feel right now determines your next step and your future path. Your past is exactly that; your past. It's over and done with.

Your future is a blank canvas, and you can paint it the way you want it to be. Yet it is how we exist today that creates the outcome of our future. Each day is an opening for a new life. Present love through: your thoughts, feelings, words, and actions. Be aware of your surroundings- but pick and choose your battles.

Think before you give your power away. Once you give it away the consequences can move you away from your values. If you are not moving towards your values, then you are moving away from them. You have to break yourself from that cycle and allow your values to guide your path forward.

We should always be moving towards what we value most in life. Before you let the words leak from your lips- or, before you take an action. Ask yourself, is it in accordance with your values, and think about what the consequences will be. When words are orchestrated and articulated in the right way they can change someone's view or alter someone's belief system. In that do or die moment you have the power to pick someone up from the lows of life or destroy someone's being just using words.

Values guide us in the direction we want to move in. They help us stay focused. They can also help provide us with stability. Values give us strength when our lives seem out of focus. It gives us meaning and holds us accountable.

Mindfulness is described as carrying out actions with understanding and control. We have anticipation of regaining a complete and meaningful life. Mindfulness helps us focus more on listening, and being understanding. Understanding not only of ourselves but of others as well. Mindfulness requires vigilance.

Be conscious of whether you start doubting your ability to be mindful and attentive. Prepare to reclaim control and seek advice when needed. The key element is to be mindfully aware; and stay focused on your values and goals.

We cannot base our self-worth on the opinion of others. You should only be in competition with yourself. You want to be the best "you" at all times. Constantly improving, learning from your mistakes, taking accountability, and moving forward. Take care of your spirit, mind, and body.

Healing: Let that shit go! Heal before moving forward.

I had to go deeper to truly understand my hurt and find my purpose and how I would define myself moving forward, not only in my relationships but in my pursuit of education and employment.

People fall victims of toxic relationships and unhealthy love, and some people choose the wrong love, one-sided love, abusive love, or they settle eventually, then get drained and become empty. What matters is how you come out on the otherside. You cant change the past. Don't hold your self hostage. Learn from the expierence.

Don't self sabatoge or feel that you are not worthy of love. You have to draw your own line and not allow people to overstep your boundries. The love you deserve is out there.

It's okay to feel anger but just make sure you're not masking anger to cover other emotions. It's okay feel anger allow yourself to process through it for a set amount of time but don't dwell on it. Having anger doesn't hurt the person who caused it unless you react in it. Have a conversation and always explain how you feel. If they want forgiveness give it to them so that you yourself will be free.

Don't be too quick to get into another relationship for fear of what people will think of you. The best time for you to heal and recollect is when you're single. It gives you time to sort your feelings and understand your emotions, and it aids in self-reflection and self-improvement.

My Dear Hubby,

The sight of you makes time stand still. You are not only my husband, but my best friend, soul mate, and everything good to my mess. You keep me grounded. I can't imagine breathing without you by my side.

You were a God sent. When I felt like my world was coming to an end and I was questioning my purpose. There you were- the light that illuminated my journey. You loved all of me and everything that came with me. No questions asked! You were there patiently waiting for my broken heart to heal. You offered me unconditional love, support, and friendship.

My desire was to love and to be in love. I'm blessed to say I know what true unconditional love feels like - to receive and to give. The love you have bestowed upon the kids and I can never be measured.

I love you more than words, more than life. I'm forever grateful for your love and am honored to be your wife.

Love you until I take my last breath and beyond,

The Mother-Ship

Live Your Best Fucking Life

Live Life. Capture moments that make your heartstrings play.

Spark random conversations and make people smile and laugh.

Always show love no matter what!

Never let fear hold you back. Stand up to it and kick fear's ass!

Write your best fucking story, the way you want it written. Never let someone else narrate your story for you.

With Love,

~Arena Horn~

SHITS & GIGGLES

1. He really loves you if he helps you take out your hair extensions.

2. I'm not going to go to the other room to fart.

3. I will pop the pimple on your back, but only if you pop mine first.

4. I know it's been three weeks. I promise I will shave next month.

5. Let me pick that boogie out of your nose.

6. I know we just woke up, but I'm going to deep throat kiss you anyways. I want to share my morning breath with you (insert duck lips here).

7. I love when we slow dance in the kitchen.

8. I love how you still look at me lovingly, even when I'm ugly crying.

9. Come look at this fucking Godzilla turd.

10. Smell my feet. Do they stink?

11. Why are you always trying to color coordinate our outfits?

12. Stop petting me like a dog.

13. I'm going to twerk up the stairs for you.

14. If you don't make a decision, I'm going to starve to death!

15. My feet are cold. I need to warm them on your back.

16. You're going to be in need of supervision for the rest of your life.

17. Legit, I miss you when you're gone.

18. I love that feeling I still get when I see you. It's either love or I need to shit.

19. I love that you kiss me when I'm ugly crying.

20. I love that you helped me put the pieces back together.

THE SHITS & GIGGLES OF LOVE

1. He really loves you if he helps you take out your hair extensions.

2. I'm not going to go to the other room to fart.

3. I will pop the pimple on your back, but only if you pop mine first.

4. I know it's been three weeks. I promise I will shave next month.

5. Let me pick that boogie out of your nose.

6. I know we just woke up, but I'm going to deep throat kiss you anyways. I want to share my morning breath with you (insert duck lips here).

7. I love when we slow dance in the kitchen.

8. I love how you still look at me lovingly, even when I'm ugly crying.

9. Come look at this fucking Godzilla turd.

10. Smell my feet. Do they stink?

11. Why are you always trying to color coordinate our outfits?

12. Stop petting me like a dog.

13. I'm going to twerk up the stairs for you.

14. If you don't make a decision, I'm going to starve to death!

15. My feet are cold. I need to warm them on your back.

16. You're going to be in need of supervision for the rest of your life.

17. Legit, I miss you when you're gone.

18. I love that feeling I still get when I see you. It's either love or I need to shit.

19. I love that you kiss me when I'm ugly crying.

20. I love that you helped me put the pieces back together.

About the Author

I'm a Midwestern–born and raised wife and mother of three. I love my alpha male, who is the calm to my storm. I'm privileged to be a teacher, protector, provider, and completely in love with my seeds. I have three fur babies that make my world go round. I love spending time with my family and friends, and I love to travel and experience new places.

I have been gifted the honor of Fairy Godmother to a young lady with intellectual disabilities. I provide respite care for several kiddos with emotional disturbances.

Made in the USA
Lexington, KY
24 October 2019